# Pipeline's
# AFRICAN ADVENTURE

By Spanky Macher
illustrations by Tim Williams

Pipeline's African Adventure

Copyright © 2023 by Spanky Macher



ISBN 978-0-9988090-8-3

"Mom! Dad! I just saw Jacob at the skate park and he invited me over to hang with him tonight. He wants me to meet his friend, Momma Kellie. She's from Chicago and is building a school in Africa. Can I go, please?" called out Pipeline, as he ran into the kitchen.

"Sure, you can go to Jacob's. Will you be
riding your bike over?" asked Dad.

"Yes, I'll ride my bike over. Thanks, Dad!" Pipeline answered.

"Be sure you pack your pajamas and wear
your helmet." said his mother.

"I can't wait to meet Momma Kellie!" Pipeline
exclaimed, while throwing the ball to Jacob.

"Hi guys!" says Jenny Webb, while rounding the corner. "Can I join in?"

"Hey kids! It's time for dinner." says Jacob's mother.
"Hi Jenny! Will you stay for dinner? Momma Kellie is here
and she has a story she wants to share with us."

"I want to tell you about my trip to Africa last year." Momma Kellie told them. "I met a Tanzanian man, Gabriel, who had a dream to educate the children in his village so that they could have a better life."

Pipeline, Jacob, and Jenny listened to stories about Africa long into the night. She told them that she lives in Chicago and goes to Africa to work with the Maasai. She's the founder of the O'Brien School for the Maasai in Tanzania.

"I want to go to Africa with you, Momma Kellie. I want to help!" exclaimed Pipeline. "So do I!" shouted Jacob and Jennie at the same time. Everyone laughed.

Momma Kellie was delighted to learn that they wanted to go to Africa to help the children and the school.

"I would love for all of you to come along with me. I would love to share this experience with you, and in turn, we will share our joy with the other villagers."

The next morning, as Pipeline was riding home, he was thinking
of ways to help the children. "What can I do that is special?"
He thought to himself. "Think, Pipeline, think." In a flash, it came
to him. He loved to play soccer and burst into joy, as he said
aloud, "That's it, I will build a soccer field for the children."

Pipeline came running into the kitchen. "How was your night with Momma Kellie, son?" asked Pipeline's mother as he rushed into the house. Pipeline was beyond excited and was telling his parents everything he had learned, without stopping to take a breath.

"Slow down, son!" said his father, "Start at the beginning and tell us everything."

"Momma Kellie is amazing!" Pipeline took a breath and continued, "She has a school in Africa. It's called the O'Brien School for the Maasai. She invited Jacob, Jenny, and me to go with her and help her at the school. I want to build a soccer field for the children." Pipeline was so excited! "Oh, Dad! I know that if I build a soccer field for the children at the school, they will be very, very happy. What do you think?"

Pipeline paced around the backyard while
his parents discussed the idea.

Pipeline's parent's called him back in. "Pipeline, we have spoken with Momma Kellie, as well as Jacob and Jenny's parents." said Dad, "We all agree that this would be a very valuable experience for all of you. You can go to the O'Brien School with Momma Kellie"

Pipeline was beyond excited. He ran into the kitchen to call Jacob and Jenny to share the good news.

A little later, Pipeline found his mother in the kitchen baking cookies. "Now son," said his mother in a serious tone, "this trip needs to be planned well. You will need to raise some money to help pay for your trip. You should do something special for the children."

Pipeline thought for a moment and said, "We could do a fundraiser at school. I can also ask Spanky for extra shifts at the restaurant, as well. Maybe he will be interested in sponsoring us?"

That evening when Pipeline was working at Spanky's, he told Spanky about his upcoming trip to Africa, and that he wanted to build a soccer field for the Maasai children at the O'Brien School.

"Wow!" exclaimed Spanky, "That is so kind of you, Pipeline! Giving back and helping others is a very important experience for you and your friends. I am proud of your efforts to help Momma Kellie. Have you thought about asking your friends to donate their sneakers so the children can have real sneakers to play soccer in?" asked Spanky.

"What a wonderful opportunity for you." said Spanky. "I would love to help you make some extra money for your trip." Spanky shook Pipeline's hand and continued, "How about I hire your friends, Jacob and Jenny, so they can earn their trip money too? I want to do more by matching your pay dollar for dollar as a donation." Pipeline was elated!

Jenny and Jacob met at Pipeline's house the next day to practice their soccer moves for their upcoming trip. Pipeline raised his arm in excitement and shouted, "You know guys, tomorrow we are working extra shifts at Spanky's to raise money for our trip. Isn't that awesome?"

The next day before their shift, they sat down with Spanky to discuss how they were going to collect enough sneakers. Spanky had a suggestion, "You can make some fliers and put them out with some large collection boxes around the school for the students to put their sneakers in." "Yes!" exclaimed Jacob. "That's exactly what we will do!"

Spanky went behind the counter and made everyone large milkshakes and passed them around. "Congratulations kids, you're on your way to Africa. Well done!"

The next day at school, Pipeline, Jacob, and Jenny put up fliers and asked their friends to donate their extra sneakers for the children at the O'Brien School so they could play soccer, and not in their bare feet. It did not take long for the enthusiasm to catch on.

Even the principal at Bloomberg High School was overjoyed
with the success of the project. He was very proud of his
student's contributions. "What a great way to start your
trip." Principal Weber said to the kids. "Congratulations!"

The next few weeks were very busy for the kids. They were juggling school and work. No time to play, but it was worth it because they were leaving for Africa the next day. They were packed and ready.

Pipeline, Jacob, and Jenny were headed to board their plane when they noticed that the tarmac was lined up with family and friends. Principal Weber, Penelope, Ed, and Matthew, to name a few, were waving farewell and wishing them a safe journey. It seemed like everyone from Boomberg High School was there to wish us well. Pipeline looked at his friends, smiled and said, "Life doesn't get any better than this!"

The trio slept during the long flight and when they woke, they discovered that they had landed. "We're here!" exclaimed Jacob. "We're here!" chimed Jenny. Pipeline joined in, "Yes! Finally! Look at everyone waving to us. There is Momma Kellie and the Franciscan Sisters. Here we are!" All three waved back through the window.

We arrived at the school and Momma Kellie was there to greet us.
She was happy to see us and shook all of our hands, welcoming us.

Pipeline is besides himself and tells Momma Kellie, "We
are so happy to be here and be involved with this
great school. Thank you for the opportunity."

Pipeline shows Momma Kellie the boxes of sneakers that they brought for the children. She was overwhelmed with appreciation.

They worked hard all day but finished the first soccer field.
They had to push the cows and donkey's off the field but once
everything was finished, they all agreed it was a great day.

The big day had arrived. The soccer field was
complete and it was time to pass out all of the
sneakers they brought and play some soccer!

Pipeline, Jacob and Jenny spent the day out in the field playing soccer with the children. It was such a magical day. They saw that the children knew how to play soccer very well.

Before they knew it, it was time to go home. As they boarded
the plane, they were happy to be going home, yet sad to leave.

They made many new friends and memories for
a lifetime. Thank you to Momma Kellie.

They finally arrived home. Their friends and family were there to greet them on the tarmac. There was a band and people were dancing and throwing confetti everywhere. Pipeline looked at this friends and said, "What a great trip we all had, but I can't wait to eat some french fries."

On January 29, 2007, my son Roland and I went to Africa to meet Kellie O'Brien. It was a monumental trip. This was the first time that Kellie, Roland, and myself were to see the O'Brien School building. The year prior, Kellie and her daughter Heather laid out the plans. It took almost a year to make it a reality. I will never forget the drive in a long, dry field with very little road that led us to the school. When we saw it, we all had tears of joy and happiness in our eyes.

Roland had collected about 200 pairs of sneakers from friends and students at Roanoke Catholic High School and it was our goal to help Kellie with her projects, as well as build a soccer field. We felt that no matter how rich or poor you are, when you are involved in either sports or music, you will find peace and happiness.

So we were able to build a soccer field, thus called "Macher Field of Dreams".

We did not have enough sneakers for the whole student population at the school, but it was the beginning of a program that has continued on for many years to follow.

Roland and I were honored by Gabriel, the village leader, by making us members of their Maasai community. Roland was given the title of Warrior and I was given the honor of an Elder, which was given to an older person, representing the specter of light and wisdom.

When the students had time to play, it was like watching a world cup of soccer. They knew the game, the rules, and most importantly, they had fun.

My inspiration over the years has been to continue to develop the program at the school, and today in 2022, it is well known in the area, with our quality fields, uniforms, and players.

O'Brien School class of 2022. The soccer team is holding
up their first ever uniforms for their soccer team.

The O'Brien School 6 and 7th grade soccer team.
They love to play soccer and they are very good.

# O'BRIEN SCHOOL FOR THE MAASAI

"THE MOST POSITIVE FACTOR IN MY LIFE IS THE O'BRIEN
SCHOOL DIFFERENCE; MEANING A STRONG BASE OF
EDUCATION, LEADERSHIP, AND DEDICATION."
-Isaya Solomon- O'Brien School Graduate, Current Form
2 Student at Orkaolili Secondary School

## ON A MISSION TO EMPOWER AND INSPIRE

Our mission is to bring an empowered future to a Maasai Community
and others within the Hai District by offering a high standard primary
with an emphasis on moral character formation for the children, as well as
entrepreneurial skills-building programs for women. Our goal is to inspire the
next generation to become leaders of Tanzania, Africa, and the world.

****100% of my book sales will be donated to the O'Brien School for the Maasai****

If you would like to learn more about the O'Brien School or make a donation,
Please visit our website: https://www.obrienschool.org

## SPONSOR   DONATE   LEARN   VOLUNTEER

O'Brien School For The Maasai*OBSM*527 Hinsdale, IL 60521
Telephone Number: +1.630.654.2291/Email: hello@obrienschool.org

# BIOGRAPHY

Roland "Spanky" Macher is a father of three successful young adults. He's a visionary and an entrepreneur. His is a spirited rebel who is creative, inspirational, and loves to be able to help others. He's a mentor and a friend who has a heart as big as they come.

He has developed a strong passion and love for the Maasai village and the O'Brien School. He visits often and provides continued support to the school and students.

Roland "Spanky" Macher with some of the younger students on Macher Field of Dreams.